BODY

WHERE YOU BELONG

OTHER BOOKS BY
CHRIST JOHN OTTO

An Army Arising:
Why Artists Are on the Frontline of the Next Move of God

Bezalel
Image of God
Yellow Book of Poetic Theology for Artists

Mary
Honor and Value
Blue Book of Poetic Theology for Artists

Drip

BODY

WHERE YOU BELONG

———

CHRIST JOHN OTTO

Body, Where you Belong
Red Book of Poetic Theology for Artists.
by Christ John Otto
Copyright © 2020 Christ John Otto, Boston, Massachusetts, all rights
reserved.

Hardcover ISBN: ISBN: 978-1-7360346-6-8
Paperback ISBN: 978-1-7360346-7-5
E-pub ISBN: 978-1-7360346-8-2

Library of Congress Control Number: 2020921723

To Murray and Martha,
Jim and Lisa,
Mara and Maureen,
and all the friends
who gathered around
the Belonging House Table.

Special thanks to
Courtney McDonald,
Nancy Mari,
Peter Lane,
Sheenagh Ash,
and Jörn Lange
for their invaluable help
in editing, providing feedback,
and preparing this
manuscript for publication.

CONTENTS

MYSTERY

If you work in a hospital,
or do counseling,
or hear confessions,
you begin
to discover
that this faith is a lot more
mysterious than you once thought.
People trust you with their secrets,
and they tell you things
that they would never tell someone else.

Aside from the typical boring stuff,
you know,
sin,
people tell you about
their spiritual experiences.
Things that,
it is assumed,
do not happen
in the "modern" world.

You soon learn
that there are a lot of people
who have seen angels,
heard the voice of God,
been visited by dead relatives,

talked to Mary,
and seen saints.

And these folks,
other than for the
hard to explain encounter
they experienced,
are generally
well-adjusted,
successful,
and responsible.
They aren't crack-pots
or religious fanatics.
They are
just men and women
who
for maybe
a brief moment
saw the veil pulled back,
and witnessed something that boggles the mind.

And by and large,
these encounters
over-ride denominations,
theological traditions,
and even personal beliefs and prejudices.

There is a reality beyond our senses.
And people encounter it fairly often.

When I was the
Assistant to the Dean of the Chapel
at Asbury,
I heard one of these
mysterious,
category busting,
but completely Biblical,
stories.

During the Pre-Seminary orientation for new students,
we hosted a series of special chapels,
and the last one was always
what Asbury and the Methodists called
"Word and Table."
For full disclosure,
I was not a Methodist.
My church called this the Eucharist.
You might have called it Holy Communion
or the Lord's Supper.

I digress.

That September,
a man had come to seminary
after having an encounter with God
through something called the Emmaus Walk.
It was an intense three day retreat
where he had a clear encounter with Jesus,
and he believed he had received a call to the ministry.
And he decided to come to seminary.

His wife did not.

Even so,
they sold their home,
quit their jobs,
and moved to Kentucky,
because
sometimes you do things you don't agree with,
because you love someone.
And this woman loved her husband.

So during the last chapel of the
Pre-Seminary Orientation
this couple sat up in the balcony.
The wife of the new student
wasn't so sure about this,
and was looking the place over.
And it came time to come forward

and receive
the Bread and Cup,
and this couple made their way down from the balcony,
and up the central aisle of the chapel.

As they made the slow way forward,
the woman looked up,
and she didn't see the
Dean of the Chapel,
or anyone else.
She looked up and saw Jesus.

And Jesus was breaking pieces
of Himself off his own body,
and placing those broken pieces
into the hand of each person who came forward
to receive.

And she began to weep,
because although she was a Methodist,
she was not a Christian,
and she quietly resented
what her husband had decided to do.

When she took the bread
from the hand of Jesus,
she received His own Body,
and also received eternal life.

The story of her life,
and her marriage,
all changed that day
at Asbury.

She knew Jesus in the breaking of the bread.
She was a woman
who was blind,
but now can see.

How she saw
I do not know.
It's a mystery.

This book is about
the mystery of
how God
chose
Bread and Wine
to be the vehicle,
for his Body and Blood.
And how art and food make
us who we are.
There are a million books
on this topic,
but none from
this point of view.

Hopefully
this book
will change your life,
and you will find,
that one of the greatest secrets
of the Christian life
is hidden
in plain sight.

THE POINT

The whole point of the Christian life is this:

To sit down with the Father
around a table
and have dinner
together as a redeemed and restored family.

Really.

The Bible is a tapestry,
and if you follow one thread, you can find that thread
woven through the entire story.

And this thread,
the "having dinner with God thread"
is probably the most important and the most prominent.
And also the most ignored
or misunderstood thread
in the Bible.

If you miss this theme,
you will miss what's really going on.

The Father wants to eat and drink with you
as an intimate member of his family.

That's a bold statement.
Let's make another one.

Many throughout history
and I mean famous, influential, powerful, and important men
missed this point completely.

The God of the Bible is
the Most Relational Being in the Universe.
He is a good Father,
and you are his child.
He is also the King of the Kingdom
and his desire from before the foundation of the world
was to do anything to have a close intimate fellowship
with you.
And that fellowship for Him
is most fully expressed as fellowship around the table.

The rest is just details.

                                    I know that you don't believe me.
                          Trust me, I have two degrees in Theology.

You were formed by religious traditions that emphasized other things.
These are your grids.

We all have them.
And for full disclosure
I spent over a decade
preparing to become
a member of the clergy.
There are a lot of influences in my slow cooker—
Sacramental, Scriptural, and Supernatural.

                                               These are my grids.
And it's good to be honest about them.
There are a lot of dishonest Christian writers
in the world today
who hide their grids

in the hope
of converting you
to their
camp.

So back to the main point:
eating and drinking with God.

Jesus said that if you have seen him,
you have seen the Father.
And that he only did what he saw the Father doing.

The last thing Jesus did
before he died
was take bread,
and wine
and eat it with his friends.
The Father must have been doing it
if Jesus did it.

I think the most important day in the life of Jesus
was the day he walked out of the tomb.
The twenty-fourth chapter of Luke
gives us details of what happened that day.

Jesus met two people on the road to Emmaus.
And it says that "he opened their minds to understand the scriptures."
He did not try to convince them with human intellect or reason.
He opened their minds with the light of the Holy Spirit.
And beginning with Genesis,
he walked them through the scriptures,
and every place that spoke of him.

And if you have missed the point,
and operated out of the wrong grid,
you will separate what Jesus says from what he DOES.
Jesus is the Incarnation.
God in the Flesh.

You will get into big trouble
when you separate his words from his actions.
He IS the Word.
The actions and the talking are one.

I don't think Jesus began
by recounting the Fall of Adam and Eve
when they walked along the road.
I believe he began with Melchizedek
who offered bread and wine to God Most High.
He talked about the Prophet
Moses speaks of in Deuteronomy.
He talked about the Manna in the wilderness.
And then he connected the sacrifices
and the restoration of relationships,
and the feasting in the Presence of God in the Tabernacle.
He reminded them that his ancestor David
was permitted to eat the Bread of the Presence
without fear or harm.
He told them about the Suffering Servant
and the promise to eat with him
on the Holy Mountain in Isaiah.
Maybe he reminded them
about the days that he
fed 4000 and 5000.
Where he took bread,
gave thanks,
broke the bread,
and gave it to his disciples.
And all the recounting
climaxed in the breaking of the bread.
And it says they KNEW HIM in the breaking of the bread.

In fact,
Luke says that
they testified
three times
that they knew him in the breaking of the bread.

Whenever the Bible repeats itself,
pay attention.

So back to the main point.

The Father wants to eat and drink with you
in restored fellowship
around the table,
as a family.

To some degree,
the early church understood this.

This is why the feeding of the multitude
is mentioned in all the gospels.
That's why Melchizedek
is mentioned in the letter to the Hebrews
And is referenced all over the early church writings.

That's also why the church
existed for more than 20 years before the first book
of the New Testament was written.
Paul, years before he wrote
I Corinthians 11
handed down to them in person what he says,
"he received from the Lord" himself. (I Corinthians 11:23)
And why, in the letter he wrote
he had to correct them
on how they
ate and drank together.

It was all about eating and drinking
in the Presence of the Father.
Maybe what you thought were the basics,
aren't.

This book is about Bread and Wine.
And it's a book for artists and creative people.
Because you are called to keep the Word and flesh together.

In the early church they began their meal
with a prayer over the bread and wine.
The prayer began with one word
Eucharistos (or its variants).
It means:
WE GIVE THANKS.

I will call this meal by this,
its most ancient name:
Eucharist.

We give thanks.

It was never about your sin,
and how bad we messed things up.
It was about giving thanks
that we could eat and drink together as a family,
in the Presence of the Father.

RETURN

With God
everything is personal.

So if the point
is to sit down with the Father
and eat with him
in complete fellowship,
we need to talk about how we got here.

You know,
broken relationships,
enmity between the sexes,
and splintering among the Body of Christ.
Because in truth,
we can't seem to eat with one another,
let alone eat with the Father.

Original sin
is the breaking of relationship.
It is the severing of the relationship between God and Adam.
It then severed the relationship between Adam and Eve.
And then our First Parents
became enemies of the creation,
and on,
and on,
and on.

Murders, wars, strife, and struggle
were the logical outcomes of this breaking.

This is the original sin.
In one of the prayers for communion
that my church used
there is this line:
"Through prophets and sages,
you called us to return."

Return to what?
Return to God.
Come back to Me.

I am going to use a word
again and again
in this book:
inadequate.

We need a reformation.
We need it because
most of the concepts
taught in the church today
have been dumbed down
and oversimplified
to the point where they do not have
their original meaning anymore.

The world is sick
but the medicine has been watered down.

God is the Most Relational Being in the Universe.
Any concept of theology
that leaves out the personal
relational aspect of God
is inadequate.

So we are prevented
from sitting down with the Father

at his table,
because of the original sin:
breaking of relationship.

But we are creatures of infinite need.
We have real needs:
real pains,
real traumas,
real longings,
that only God can fill.

And so
throughout history,
people have tried to meet those needs.
Sex,
drugs,
idols,
witchcraft,
magic,
and a million little bad habits.

And the Father,
just like that scene in the Garden,
calls to us,
"Where are you?"

"Return to Me."

This word,
in Hebrew,
is the word Shuv.

It is the root of the word "teshuvah."
Teshuvah is the word for repentance.
To turn around.

In Exodus 24
we get the one of the most important

"eating and drinking with God"
scenes in the Bible.
Moses,
and seventy of the elders of Israel
go up on the mountain
and they see God face to face.
And it says that God did not lay a hand on them,
and that they ate and drank
with God
on the mountain.

God
right there in the Old Testament,
wanted a relationship.

Return to me.
This is one side of repentance.
The turning.

And yes,
it is turning away from sin and separation
from God.

But more importantly,
it is turning towards Someone.

It is not enough to grieve your sin,
feel sorry and regret.
It's not enough to break your nasty habit.
And it is not enough to stop doing something in your own strength.
You must turn to the Lord.
You must come and be reconciled to God,
and then,
you must be reconciled to one another.
This is the goal,
full stop.

Dinner with the Father.

It is all about relationship.

So the Prophet Hosea
in the context of the
broken
relationship
he has with his wife,
a prostitute,
says:

Come,
let us return to the Lord;
for he has torn us, that he may heal us;
he has stricken, and he will bind us up.

In another place Hosea
pleads with them to RETURN to the Lord.

It's about relationship.
It's about an invitation.
And yes,
it is about sin.
But not about the rotten things we have done,
but about our separation from God.
Everything else is a symptom of the separation.

It is always about God.
When we get fixated on our sin,
it becomes about us.

In the community house
where I have a room
we sometimes have
intense discussions after dinner.
And recently we
talked about the fundamental difference
between communities that celebrate the Eucharist weekly,
and those that do not.

In the end
it boils down to this:
who is at the center of the activity in the service?
Is it God centred,
or man centred?

I will let you ponder that.

Return to Me.

And Jesus
came preaching the Kingdom of God,
saying "repent" for the Kingdom of heaven is near.

You could put this verse
in the mouth of any of the prophets:

Come unto Me,
you who are weary,
and heavy laden,
and I will give you
rest.

Take my yoke upon you,
and learn from me,
for I am meek and lowly,
and my yoke is easy
and my burden is light.

Return to me.

In returning and rest
you shall be saved,
in quietness and confidence
shall be your strength.

Return to me.

METANOIA

Now let's talk about another aspect of repentance:
the transformation.

When we hear the word "Repent!"
We immediately think of street preachers,
people crying over their sins,
penance,
and remorse.
And because of the culture I was raised in
I seem to always remember
bleeding Jesus pictures,
and the Sorrowful Mother,
all trying to make me feel guilty.

And whenever I am with a group of leaders
who are crying out for revival
they immediately begin to think of sin
in the nation or nations,
and how the people
need to repent.
So that God
can
move.

And of course,
they are pointing to

the histories of revival,
especially the holiness
and evangelical movements
in the 19th Century.

I'm here to hopefully bring some balance to all that.
Remember,
it's all about relationship
first with the Father,
and then with one another.

The classic definition of repentance taught to people is:
"to turn around"
(but almost always
it means to turn away from sin).
Remember Shuv,
and teshuvah?
That definition of repentance in your mind,
may not be wrong
but it is inadequate.
It just doesn't reflect the fullness of meaning in the New Testament.

In the English Bible tradition,
the word that is most often translated "repent"
is the Greek word,
"metanoia."

It's a compound word,
made of a prefix and a noun
to form a verb.

Yes, even artists need to know a little grammar.

Meta means to change.
It does not mean
"to turn"
or change direction.
It simply means change.

It comes down to us in the term for how
a caterpillar becomes a butterfly:

                                            Metamorphosis.

Which, if you know Greek
is also a compound word of a noun with a prefix and a suffix:

Meta—to change

Morphe—shape or form

osis—process of.

Metamorphosis is the process of changing shape from one thing to another.

It's very simple.

The second part of this word
is also very simple.

"Noia" means mind or thinking.
The Greeks thought that thinking and the mind were one.
As you probably do as well.
Jews did not.

The way this comes to us in English is the word "paranoia."
It's a full on Greek word we all know.

"Para" is the word for come behind or come ahead, or even come along side.
It can mean both—as in paramedic—a medic who gets there first.

To be paranoid is to think someone is behind you.

                                            Creepy.

So, now that we understand the component parts
we can put the two together and we have our word
Metanoia.
To change your mind or thinking.

And intrinsic in this,
because the Hebrew mindset does not
isolate the thinking from the doing,
is the idea that your thoughts
are going to change your behaviour.

The Hebrews thought that the mind
was connected to your gut, or your bowels.
So when Jesus had compassion, it says he "felt it in his gut."
The head is never floating somewhere apart from the body.
Remember that for later.

Have you noticed something?

                                    I have not mentioned sin.
Metanoia is not about sin.
It's about change.
Metanoia is about an inside out transaction,
that is not about morality,
reparation,
or even consequences.
It's about becoming something else.
Maybe it's about becoming a new creation.

When you truly metanoia,
the sin
which is really a symptom
of the separation from God,
and
of a wrong identity,
begins to go away.
You are changed.

That's why
a lifestyle of repentance
is eternal,
but hopefully,
a lifestyle of sin
ends when you get up out of the waters of Baptism.

The difference truly is
not about your moment of decision,
but about choosing the life of a disciple.
These are two vastly different things.
God is always finding places in your thinking
that need to change.
Even if it
doesn't really add up to sin.

Turning to God
will in turn
bring a transformation of your thinking.
Turning and Transformation
must be held together.

So why all the focus on sin?

                              (And dear brothers and sisters,
                 I am not taking lightly the seriousness of sin
                              its power to keep us enslaved,
                                    its power to destroy
                                   people and nations,
                              and its power to distort
                                      our own sense
                                          of value,
                                          identity,
                                 and belonging.)

Blessed Saint Jerome
hid himself in a cave
and translated the Bible
into Latin.
He did this,
because most Christians at the time
spoke Latin,
but could not understand Greek and Hebrew.
The word for common people in that day
was "vulgar"
and so,
his Bible became known as the Vulgate.

A Bible for the common people.

One should always be careful
when you read a Bible
that is translated by one man alone.
Even if he is the greatest scholar of all time,
and Jerome was no slouch,
he will make mistakes.
No one person has an exhaustive knowledge of two of the
most complex and nuanced
languages in history.
And everyone has
blind spots.
They are products of their own cultures and ages.
So the *Message*,
The Passion Translation,
Young's Literal,
and the *Living Bible*
are all helpful,
but they should not be
the final authority.
Sometimes one person's point of view
can open your eyes,
but it cannot replace
a Bible translated by a large group
who each bring their own wisdom
and often disagreements
to the table.

Well,
Rome collapsed
more or less,
the day after
Jerome finished his Bible.

(That friends, was an example of Hyperbole,
an overstatement for effect,
not a false statement.
People need to learn the difference.)

And no one followed after Jerome
to challenge his misinterpretations
and mistakes.
Civilization was gone.
Scholars were gone.
And the church was barely holding it all together.
And Jerome's Bible became the only one
in the West
for a thousand years.
The western world relied on a Bible translated by one man.

One of Jerome's mistakes
is quite famous,
and determined the direction of Western Art.
Jerome confused the word for shining
with the word for horns.

So,
Moses had horns when he came down from the mountain.
For over a thousand years
artists portrayed Moses with horns on his head.
Oops.

Jerome
chose a word from the legal system
to translate metanoia.
The word was
"Penitentio."

This word means to pay a restitution for a crime committed.

And with that,
Jerome sowed the seeds
for the Protestant Reformation.
It was an innocent mistake,
and a subtle change in nuance,
that grew into a mighty tree.

And from then on,
Repentance would be associated
with restitution,
penance,
and sin.

And Protestants believe in penance,
they just call it consequences,
and live under self-condemnation,
and introspection.

You can't build a house
if you are always redigging the foundation.
You can't be beautiful
when you spend your life picking your scabs.

Returning to the Lord,
and then being transformed in your mind,
is a way forward.
There is no looking back.
Then you can let go of the past,
and get into the new thing God is doing.

God is always doing a new thing.

This book is really about
you changing your mind
so that you can be empowered to receive
all that God has for you
as a creative person,
and so you can enter into a life of endless becoming
so you can share that wholeness with others.

Metanoia.

Change your mind.

Listen to these familiar verses from the Bible,
with a more accurate translation:

Mark 1:15.
This is the beginning of the ministry of Jesus.
"Jesus said: 'The time has reached its fulness,
the Kingdom of God is here,
turn to God and change the way you think so your life is different,
and believe the Good News.'"

Acts 2:38
Peter at Pentecost:
"Return to the Lord and be transformed in your mind and life,
be baptised and you will receive the forgiveness of your sins,
and the gift of the Holy Spirit."

Acts 3:19-20
"Change your thinking, that your sins may be forgiven,
and times of refreshing may come from the Lord."

Paul in Romans 2:4
"It is God's kindness
that leads to a transformation in your thinking and a turning to the Lord."

It's an inside out,
transformation.

This is why Paul says in Romans 12,
"be transformed by the renewing of your mind."

He was describing metanoia.

Yes,
in the process
sin is dealt with,
through confession and receiving forgiveness.
This is not a penitential
endless state of woe,
but a simple transaction,
because Jesus already dealt with your sin,
and you can be free.

This is a process of laying aside the false identity
of sinner,
slave,
and orphan;
in exchange for your True Identity in Christ:
Holy,
Royal,
and Adopted.

When those thoughts take over,
why would you want to sin?

Metanoia.
Change your thinking,
so you can have all God
wants to lavish on you.

ANSWERS

When I was a student
I wrote in the margin of my notebook:

"These people are answering questions
no one is asking."

I now realize I was a snarky kid.
But that snarky kid was onto something.

Those unquestioned answers were a disconnect
between theology and reality.

And because of this disconnect
between the academy and reality,
my training overlooked
or ignored
many of the best bits of the Bible.

It's become my life's mission to answer the questions
that I believe people are really asking.

And the questions people are asking
point right back to our main idea:
to sit down with the Father
together at Table,
in unbroken fellowship,
and eat together.

Hopefully I can "connect the dots"
and inspire artists and creative people
to communicate this reality to the world.

All the questions being asked today,
and all the hot topics in the news,
can be boiled down to three core questions:

Do I have value?

What is my identity?

Where do I belong?

                    Yes, I say this in every one of my books.
            No one else is saying it yet, so I will keep doing it.

Five hundred years ago
a group of people attempted to
make all of Christianity an answer to one question:
"What must I do to be saved?"
And for the sake of this book,
they did this with the Eucharist.
For some of these men
the Eucharist was problematic.
In the minds of the reformers,
the Eucharist did not provide a direct answer to this question.
This,
and many other practices
of the historic church,
were removed,
or sidelined.

Remember what I said at the beginning about grids?

You see,
If the whole point of the Christian life
as I said at the beginning of this book
is to eat and drink with the Father at a table

in unbroken fellowship
with Him and other believers
forever,
then
this celebration
with bread and wine
is about something other
than what most people think it is.

It's about value and worth and belonging.

You have been invited and welcomed
by the Most Relational Being in the Universe,
to be an honored guest at his table.
And if you eat at his table,
he considers you family.
You are of supreme value.

It's about Identity.

If you eat at this Table,
you are the member of a Royal Family.
You are a Son or Daughter of God.
You are not what you do,
or defined by what you have done.
You are defined by who you are,
and you are sitting with the Father.

It's about Belonging.

You have an engraved permanent name card
and a reserved seat at this Table.
It's reserved for you.
Because you belong here,
and are welcome here,
you have unbroken fellowship
with the Host,
and all the other guests.

Again, note that I never mentioned sin
or penance
or penitence
or Repentance.

But I have mentioned transformation,
and turning,
from one reality to another.
And that will change your behavior from the inside out.

This is the reality of the New Covenant.
If you have been baptized into Jesus Christ,
the old is gone,
the new is come,
you are adopted.
You are a new creation.
And your life,
and your identity,
is formed
around a new and glorious
community:
A new family and a new Table.

And that reality is not about you
and your sin.
It's not about self-examination,
or penitence.
It's about Thanksgiving,
and it's about grace.

It's about accepting and receiving.
It's about holding out your hands
and letting someone else feed you.

This is so contrary to the "Christianity" that I encounter
that it's no surprise that
I meet people dabbling in the occult,
exploring Eastern religious practices,

and taking anti-depressants,
or worse,
to feel better.

I recently read a stunning quote from James Jordan:
"If your Christianity is not working for you,
then what you believe is not Christianity."

Either Jesus is the Truth,
and what he gave us is True,
Or, it's all hogwash
and we are all doomed
and we might as well embrace all the "-isms."

There are no limits
to what God has made available to us.
And the most limitless thing available to us is
grace.

DYNAMIC GRACE

The conventional beliefs
that I hear people repeat,
again and again,
are not wrong or incorrect.
They are inadequate.
They just don't go far enough.

There's that word again:
inadequate.

Take for example,
the basic protestant evangelical definition of grace:

Grace is undeserved favor.

That is not wrong.
But based on the New Testament,
it is a very weak definition.
It is not adequate.
It is also pretty stiff,
and it is impersonal.
There is nothing in the gospel that is impersonal.
Remember, we are talking about the Most Relational Being in the Universe.

So,
again for full disclosure,
we need to define terms.

In the Universal Church, there are only two ways to understand grace.

The understanding of grace that emerged during the reformation
and now dominates some sections of the protestant church
is an abstract, static, and legal understanding.
It was designed and developed
as a reaction to the real abuses
just prior to the last reformation.
It was a new grid against an old one.

This understanding of grace
is usually described with the following illustration—

Imagine that you are in a law court.
You are guilty of murder,
and you are going to the gallows.
And just before the judge drops his gavel,
and pronounces your sentence,
someone comes out of the crowd,
and presents himself to the judge.
And that person offers to die in your place,
as your substitute,
and you are set free—
even though we all know
that you are a dirty rat.

That act, and this scene,
is grace.
And it is.

It rests on an understanding of the Bible
as a book about legal justification.
You are guilty,
and before God,
you ought to go to hell.
And you don't
because Jesus
chose to be your substitute.

It is totally undeserved,
you dirty rat.

It is no surprise that this idea took hold,
since John Calvin was a lawyer.
He wasn't a priest or a pastor before the Reformation.
I think that is important to recognize.
He didn't love the sheep the way a shepherd does.

And because of this
there are a few problems with the courtroom metaphor.

First,
God is the Judge.
And in this court,
He doesn't like his job,
and he really doesn't like criminals.
So he is always frowning at you.
And it is only because of Jesus,
the substitute for you,
you dirty rat,
that he doesn't zap you
in the cosmic bug zapper.
This god would probably like to zap you,
because of the funny noise you would make.
Zap!

(Yes, I know I shouldn't be making light of this,
but the lies Satan uses to keep people bound
should be mocked endlessly.
And by the way, I call this lie
"God is mad and I am bad.")

And here is another problem,
It's static.
It is an abstract state,
without a way to experience it in an Incarnational way,
except through mental agreement.
Remember the disconnect between thinking and doing?

37

And it's very inadequate.

What happens when you leave the court room?
Do you go out and murder again?
Do you live in fear of the angry judge forever?
Do you spend your life
trying
to be a better person
on your own
now that you are free
when in your mind you can hear that bug zapper in the distance?
And so deep down,
you are always thinking you need to repent for something.
zap
zap
zap

I know many people who live life this way.
They are not very happy, but they smile and say they are Christians.
They are nice, but not loving.
There is no rest,
only performance,
self-examination,
a dull anxiety,
and fear.

And this is where the reformation grid understanding of grace,
this shapeless,
impersonal,
somewhat limited,
understanding of grace,
lets you down.

You get trapped between remorse and trying harder.

Zap!

It's why so many people who believe this
eventually embrace some form of universalism
with a shapeless, formless, powerless god.

The only way to relax is to unplug the bug zapper,
and live any way you want.

It is why people who come from this world get disappointed with God.

This legal concept of grace
is only one facet of something much bigger.

The rest of Christianity—
including the Apostolic Fathers
from the early church,
the Catholics and the Orthodox,
the Wesleyan movements,
the pentecostal and charismatic movements,
and modern revivalists
—believes in dynamic grace.

Dynamic grace is dangerous
and it can be abused.
Those who believe in static grace often refer to it as "hyper-grace."
But,
this kind of grace
is the kind that really changes lives.

For most of Christian history,
and among the vast majority of Christians,
grace has been understood as something
that is moving
can be received,
can be experienced and felt,
and encountered in life transforming ways.

And this kind of grace is personal,
not based in legal or philosophical arguments,
and it is messy.

Dynamic Grace is the Person, Power, and Presence of Jesus Christ,
experienced through the work of the Holy Spirit.

So Paul could write:
"In Him we live, and move, and have our being."

And John Wesley could say,
"My heart was strangely warmed."

And Saint Francis could see and hear Jesus say:
"Francis, come rebuild my church."

John the Beloved could say:
"This grace appeared,
we have seen it,
and we have touched it."

Grace is Jesus Christ.
If you have seen Jesus,
you have seen grace.
And if you have seen Jesus,
then you have seen the Father.

So back to the parable of the law court.

You are pronounced guilty.
But, this time,
rather than Jesus being your substitute,
Jesus is your Advocate,
through the Holy Spirit
He fights for you and pleads your case.
He presents his wounds to the Judge and says,
"See,
I have already paid the penalty for this crime,
and I am alive.
I have completed this work,
and this criminal doesn't deserve it.
My Person, Presence, and Power has brought justice.
And now I am going to go out the door
with this free person,
and I am going to stay with them

and we are going to become family
and my Person, Presence, and Power is going to
bring a transformation
in every area of their life."

There is no reason to fear the judge,
because now the judge is smiling
and you are promised
you will never have to revisit
the courtroom again.
You see,
the Judge,
is your Father,
and he has been wanting the very best for you,
from the beginning.

It is for freedom,
that Christ has set you free.

This is grace,
real,
living,
incarnational,
transformative,
personal,
grace.

And here is the rub.

The New Testament
gives us practical ways to regularly
re-experience this grace.
It is not theory.
There are established ways
Jesus said
would be the ways we could experience him.
We call these things
"Means of Grace."

Prayer,
fellowship with others,
the Bible,
Worship,
and giving thanks over bread and wine and eating it together
(as well as Baptism and the laying on of hands for healing).

These are the ways the Bible says
we can access
the Person, Presence, and Power of Jesus
through the Holy Spirit.
Grace is something you can experience,
not just think about or
believe in.

And this might surprise you.
We are still talking about
"What must I do to be saved?"
Because salvation
is not about being legally justified.
Salvation is about becoming fully human,
being transformed from one
degree of glory
to another.
You will never stop being saved.

That's good news.
It is deceptively simple.
It is no longer about what you do,
or what you intellectually agree with or understand,
but about who you are becoming.

It is no longer about your effort.
It is about rest,
and identity,
and value,
and belonging.

SACRIFICE

Wherever I speak on Bezalel,
I always ask a question of my audience.
"Why did God command that they put salt on all of the sacrifices?"

And since my audiences are mostly artists and creative people,
the answers are very creative
and wrong.

"Salt doesn't burn."
"Salt is a preservative."
"Salt is a symbol of holiness."
"It's a prophetic foretelling of the Sermon on the Mount."

No one ever seems to manage the obvious,
that the sacrifices were food.
You put salt on things to make them taste better.

                                                              Duh.

I am guessing
(please forgive me if I am wrong)
that your understanding of sacrifice
goes something like this:

In the Old Testament
God was really mad.

So to keep him from killing the Israelites,
he demanded that they burn up animals
all the time
to keep him from killing them.
Because God needed something to die in order to satisfy his wrath.
And the people,
who were all dirty rotten sinners,
brought their animals
to be killed for God,
and they were all burned up
(because for some reason, God likes the smell of burning flesh)
in payment
for their sins.
And these animals were the "fines" that were required,
to keep them from being punished for their sins.
So, in this incorrect understanding of sacrifice,
the offering was a sin tax.

I should note,
that the underlying idea here
is that we are still in a law court
there is still the angry god with a bug zapper,
and no one is willing to be a substitute,
so you have to offer the Judge
bulls and goats
to hopefully put off
your trip to the gallows.
He's mad.
We're bad!
Zap!

The problem is
God is not a wild-eyed angry monster.
The nature of God does not magically change
when you flip the page in the middle of your Bible,
between the Old and New Testaments.
He is a good Father.
The problem is not the Old Testament,

the problem is the lens you are using to read it.
This law-court,
angry god analogy,
needing a substitute,
is a very big smudge
on your lens
keeping you from understanding what the Bible is all about.
It is why there are sections that don't make sense,
because substitution and justification is not what the Bible is all about.

In the Old Testament,
there is a key idea that we have lost.
Actually,
to be honest
Israel lost this key idea somewhere along the way.
We know this
because of the things the prophets say.

Words in Hebrew are very interesting things.
Each letter is really a picture.
And the pictures,
when you arrange them
sometimes tell little stories,
and define the words.
And each word is made up of a root,
and the root is very important.
It is the key idea,
and then other words are built out of that root,
like a little tree.
And all the words from one root
form little "family trees" of words.

The word "Sacrifice" in Hebrew
is the word "Qorban."
It is formed of a root of three letters, that we will transliterate
"QRB."
QRB contains a core word picture of
getting close,

being near,
and relationship.

And if you look at the "family tree"
growing from the same root as "sacrifice,"
you find the next closest relative
is the word for "family."
And after that is the word for "close."

Family, closeness, and sacrifice are all connected.

Remember our main point:

> The goal of everything is
> you sitting at table,
> and eating with your Father
> forever.

It's right here in Hebrew grammar.

So, when Bezalel the artist
was empowered by the Holy Spirit
to build and design the Tabernacle,
central to its purpose and function
was a place where people would come
on their day off,
to eat and drink together,
close to each other,
and close to God.
And the people and God would have a feast
in a replica of heaven on earth.

And very few of the sacrifices were about sin.
Actually,
the sacrifice for sin
that the book of Hebrews talks about in depth
is the Day of Atonement,
once a year.
The regular sacrifices were very different.

They were fellowship offerings,
peace offerings,
thank offerings,
wave offerings,
and purification offerings.
And only one sacrifice was meant to be "burned up" completely.
The sacrifices were salted,
because they were food.
The Altar
was a massive barbeque
designed to feed the multitudes.

And rightly so,
scholars have been astounded
at the layers of meaning
in the Tabernacle,
and how they all seem to point to Jesus.
Because all of this was pointing toward a
perfect sacrifice
for all time.
A perfect fellowship
with the Father,
the Son,
and the Holy Spirit,
and with each other,
as a new Humanity
a living body.

Even in the Old Testament,
the desire of the Father
was to sit and eat and drink with you.
He wanted to be close to you.
He wanted to come to you
in the place of rest and celebration.
The aroma that pleased God
in the sacrifices,
was the smell of a roast
over an open fire.

Just like a proud papa,
he was looking forward to sitting down at the table
with all his children
and sharing in their joys, sorrows,
dramas, and celebrations.

This is the fullest expression of the concept of sacrifice.

When I was a student
there seemed to be one discussion
that resurfaced repeatedly.
"Why did God tell Abraham
to sacrifice his son Isaac?"

                                        The reality is worse
                                and better than you thought.
First,
    based on what I have told you,
    Abraham was not only thinking he was going to have to kill Isaac,
    he also was thinking he would have to eat him.

Yes, that's right.
And other Canaanite nations did practice ritual cannibalism.

Second,
Abraham knew
that if God was asking him to make a sacrifice,
it was because God wanted to get close to Abraham,
and be his friend.
And Abraham
wanted to be God's friend.
And somehow,
Abraham had a sense
that even if he had to eat Isaac,
it was going to work out somehow,
because great things happen when you are God's friend.
And somehow
just the act of taking Isaac up the mountain

was an act of faith,
and out of that,
God revealed a part of his own nature and ways.
"The LORD will Provide."

And when we come to the New Testament,
Jesus is presented as the "Lamb of God."
He is born in the house of bread, Bethlehem.
He is laid in a manger, a feeding trough.
And he dies at the time when the Passover lambs are sacrificed in the Temple.

Yes, there are a lot of food metaphors going on.

Remember the point?
It's all there,
layer
upon layer
upon layer.

Yes,
Jesus did die for our sin.
But he also died
as an offering to restore
fellowship,
closeness,
and a relationship
with the Father.
He was a sacrifice
in this full and wonderful sense.
Just like Isaac,
Jesus went to the mountain
realizing we would have to eat him
as the Sacrifice.

In the last chapter I talked about how insufficient
the concept of grace is for many people.
Another inadequate concept is
the concept of Substitutionary Atonement.

This is the idea that all Jesus did on the cross was die in my place.

Yes,
Jesus did die in my place,
but from his own words,
and from what he left us,
this was not his whole mission.
His face was fixed toward Jerusalem
because he was determined
to restore the fellowship
Adam once had with the Father.

And the sin
did need to be paid for,
but that was only one piece of the transaction.
He was the perfect peace offering.
He was the perfect thank offering.
He was the perfect fellowship offering.
He was the spotless,
Passover lamb,
whose blood marks us,
and who becomes a feast for us
to celebrate with the Father—
a new and complete restored family.

In my work
I meet many angry ex-catholics
for whom this idea of sacrifice is especially problematic.

If you are a good Roman Catholic,
you receive your first communion when you are about seven years old.
And the church takes this event seriously,
and doesn't want children to receive the Eucharist in an unworthy manner.
That's Biblical.
And so, for about a year,
children go prepare for their first communion.
And they are told that the Mass is a sacrifice.

And so many of these children
come to believe
(and I have even heard priests teach this)
that Jesus is re-sacrificed on the cross at every mass.

That's not Biblical.

And of course,
the dear nuns teaching these children
are attempting to instill in these little souls
the importance of what they are about to receive.
And so they try to explain Thomas Aquinas
and the teachings of the Catechism of the Catholic Church.
That we enter into the completed sacrifice
every time we receive the Eucharist.

But these kids
have in their mind,
images of pagan sacrifices in movies,
the idea of a wrathful God,
and a limited understanding of time, let alone eternity.
It's confusing,
and so these little children make sense of it
any way they can.

And that child's eye understanding of sacrifice,
becomes "the official teaching of the church."
And sadly, even some leaders never grow up and they keep teaching the
error.

Remember Metanoia?
It is about changing your mind and your beliefs,
so that you in turn live a different kind of life.

You may believe this error about sacrifice.
Today is a great day to have your mind changed,
to believe something different.
Don't be limited by the inadequate things you have heard.
Become an adult and embrace the truth.

The Eucharist
is a sacrifice.
It is a sacrifice of praise
for the victory of God in Jesus Christ.
It is a fellowship offering
where we stand together and proclaim
Worthy is the Lamb
who was slain
to receive
honor,
and power,
and glory,
and riches,
and wealth and wisdom and strength.
It is finished,
and it is complete,
and someone is fighting for you.

Sacrifice is about
presenting yourself,
and your gifts
in restored fellowship,
in a restored family,
close to God
and close to each other.

It is eating and drinking with God
in the most complete sense.

Sacrifice
is then
an expression of grace.
It is a reminder that
we have someone fighting for us
in the Presence of the Father,
so that we may never experience
distance from Him again.

It is an expression on earth
as it is and will be in heaven.
A complete and total
restoration of relationship.
The old is gone,
the new has come,
and we are close.

REMEMBER

10 years ago
we began
celebrating Passover
as a community.

In the beginning,
it was simply about
reconnecting with my own Jewish roots,
and also about
having another excuse
for a party.

I wasn't expecting it
to be life transforming,
or emotional,
or the biggest event
of our ministry year.

Passover became all of those things,
and the Belonging House Seder
got bigger and bigger.

And I worked very hard for it to stay
like family,
and Jewish.

We didn't have an educational
Christianized Seder.
We had dinner,
with plates,
and napkins,
and we used the basic Passover
service,
called a Haggadah,
with a few tweaks.

One of the rules about Passover is to invite your
non-Jewish friends to participate,
so they can hear the story.
We were very good at keeping that rule.

There are a couple places in the Service
where I still become emotional,
shed tears,
and sometimes have to compose myself.

"Our Father Abraham
was a wandering Aramean
we lived in the land of Haran,
and we worshipped idols."

"We were slaves in Egypt,
but with an outstretched arm
and a mighty hand,
Our God
brought us out,
and now we are free."

and this,
"In every generation
we must tell the story,
and remember,
as if we too were slaves
in Egypt."

In every generation,
we must act as if
we were the ones who have been freed.

That is what the Bible means,
when it says
"remember."

Remembering
is becoming reconnected
to an event in the past,
and making it a part of who you are today.

In little chapels and churches
all over the United States,
there are communion tables.
And across the front is this inscription:

THIS DO IN REMEMBRANCE OF ME.

And once a month,
usually on the first Sunday of each month,
folks gather around these tables to
remember Jesus.

But mostly,
they examine themselves
and remember their sin.

And it becomes a ritual
in reinforcing a false identity,
dirty rat,
needing a substitute.
Zap!

When Jesus said
do this in memory of me,
he said it in the context of Passover

where he and his disciples,
were remembering that they too
were once slaves in Egypt,
but with a mighty hand and an outstretched arm
God set them free.
Context is everything,
and in every generation,
the Jews reconnect with their
redemption.

And Jesus said,
My own arm will bring the victory,
I have tread the winepress alone,
and my garments are red.
I have stayed in the belly of the fish
three days,
and I am triumphant.

You are no longer dead
in your trespasses and sins
but you have died with me
and you are now raised
and seated with me
in heavenly places
above all rule and authority.

Remembering is not
an intellectual
exercise.
Remembering is being
reconnected
to your true identity,
through a retelling of a story,
and an experience around the Table.

The mind and the body
are connected.
The thinking and the doing are one.

Jesus redefined
and intensified
an annual celebration.
And from the night in Emmaus
until now,
every Sunday is Passover.
Every Sunday is the day
Jesus walked out of the tomb.
Remember.
Reconnect.
Re-enact.
Re-experience.
You were with him by the cross,
and you have heard the good news from Mary.
He is not here, he is risen.
Christ has died,
Christ is risen,
Christ will come again.

It is really not about you
and your sin.

It is about Him.

As Aristotle said,
You become what you repeatedly do.

And you become what you focus on.
And He knew that you would need to refocus at least once a week,
and you would need a constant reminder,
and you would not become who you really are,
unless you remembered,
reconnected,
re-enacted,
re-experienced,
his saving work
repeatedly.

The Greek mindset puts a barrier between the mental
and the physical.
You can believe something
and it never has to have anything to do with your life.
This is why so many Christians
think that eating a cracker once a month
is enough,
because they can think about Jesus
anytime.

Jesus was Jewish
and he knew,
your mental capacity
is an intrinsic part of your physical life.

We are often more spiritual than Jesus.

Jesus said,
take this bread
and eat it,
it is my body
given for you
and when you eat it,
eat it and remember—
reconnect
re-experience
re-enact—
Me.

It is in the doing
not the thinking
that remembering happens.

Passover
is a constant reminder
to the Jewish people,
that they exist,
and have been changed,

because of the intervention of God,
from a wandering tribe,
to an enslaved people,
and then
to a free nation.

Eucharist
is a constant reminder
to the Redeemed Believer
that they have been changed,
because of the intervention of God,
from sinners,
to saints,
a royal priesthood,
a holy nation,
and a new Creation.

It is in the doing,
that remembering happens.

SYMBOL

In the 1970's
my Aunt Cheri drove
a yellow
Volkswagen
Super Beetle
Convertible.

It was a very cool car.

And although the heat didn't work,
I thought the interior of the car
was really interesting.

Unlike the rest of my family
who drove American cars,
this car was foreign.

And instead of words on all the knobs
on the dashboard,
this car had pictures.
Little pictograms
to help indicate what the knob
was meant to do.
Volkswagen was the first
car marketed to many countries,

and it was smarter to use
pictures
instead of words.

Those pictures were symbols.

Our world is overflowing with them.

A symbol is simply
something that is used
to respresent something else.

Words are symbols for the thing
they speak of.

And some languages
are more deeply connected to their pictorial roots
than others.

The Bible takes symbols seriously.
If words are symbols,
then Jesus
the Word
becoming flesh
is a very serious idea.

When symbols get confused,
or redefined
terrible things can happen.

                                    I hope you, as a creative person,
                                            understand this.

I once knew a Christian music group that decided
to use a pentagram
for its logo.

The director of that group had a smug attitude,
and he thought he could do whatever he wanted,
"because that's just a symbol."

Imagine,
for a moment,
that you get pulled over by the police car,
for running a red stop light.

When the cop
asks you what you were doing,
is it acceptable to reply:

"Officer,
that light is just a symbol,
and I decided today red means go,
and green means stop."

        I'm sure he will be very sympathetic as he writes your ticket.

Ironically,
the world around us takes symbols more seriously
than it did even 20 years ago.
But Christians seem to think
symbols are disposable.

Let's go back to this idea
that words are symbols.
Words represent the thing
of which they speak.

Jesus himself said,
"You search the scriptures,
thinking that in them you will find life,
but you ignore the one of whom they speak."

Symbols always point to another reality.
They are not the reality,
but they point to it.
This is why color,
shape,
image,

and
gesture
all have such power
throughout history
and throughout the world.
A swastika means something.
So does a hammer and sickle.
So does a rainbow flag,
and
a middle finger.

You cannot not communicate.

Jesus knew this.

He is the Symbol.
He is the image of the Invisible God.
If you have seen him,
you have seen the Father.
And he was a symbol:
the Word.
And the Word
became a living,
breathing,
symbol.

Everything Jesus did
and everything Jesus said,
pointed to a reality beyond
what our eyes saw
and our ears heard.

And Jesus,
in all that he did,
enacted that reality before our eyes.
He was the picture
that speaks a thousand words.

And so
when Jesus says,
I am the Living Bread
that came down from heaven,
He is.
This isn't just metaphor.
It is a definition of who He is as a symbol.

I am the Living Water.
I am the Door.
I am the Way.
He is.

And every action that Jesus performed
becomes a work of art.

This is so important for us,
because our calling
in the Kingdom
is to be a reflection of that glory.

This is a Kingdom of Priests,
and this priesthood
ministers in symbol.

We pour water,
and we break bread.

We are priests of symbol.
We are working in representations of other things.
We are making the unseen visible,
just like Jesus.

He is the Icon
of the Invisible God.
A sign
and a symbol
to show us the way.

SIGN

You may be thinking,
"I thought this was a book for artists,
this book doesn't seem to be about art."

The truth is
every great artist,
no matter their particular craft,
has to be a great human being.
Part of that is being educated.
Education is the skill
of making life an endless experience of learning.
And a Kingdom artist
has to be well schooled
in all that concerns the Kingdom.
This ignorance of the Kingdom,
and life in general,
helps explain what passes for "Christian" art.
For some reason,
many Christians think it is noble
to be uneducated
and ignorant.

I digress.

And now,
I am about to connect some dots between
theology and your life as an artist.

Once upon a time,
I was a sign painter.
In fact, most of my career as an artist
has been making hand painted signs and displays for businesses.

The New Testament uses the word
"sign" for all the miracles Jesus performed.
The Greek word for sign appears seventy-seven times in the New Testament,
and most of those times are in the gospels.

Jesus was running around
making signs
to point the way.

And remember,
If you have seen Jesus,
then you have seen the Father.

Jesus was a performance artist.

Creative friend,
my hope is that
through what you do,
you will make signs as well
so that when people see your work,
they will see Jesus,
and the Father.

Of all the signs that Jesus performed,
the miracles,
there is only one that is recorded in all four gospels.
It is the feeding of the five thousand.

And if that wasn't enough,
Jesus fed four thousand on another occasion,
and that is recorded in Mark and Matthew.

And even more interesting,
this is the only miracle
that Jesus takes the time to explain and interpret.

That seems pretty important,
don't you think?

Remember what I said about the lens
you use to read the Bible.
If you read it with the wrong lens,
you will miss what is happening.

When you read to find support for your theology,
or read to support your doctrine,
or read to find some moral teaching,
or read to find the "moral" like Aesop,
you will miss what's really happening.
You will be unable to observe the unexpected,
or see details that really are important.

                                     Pride makes you blind.
                 Religious pride makes you double blind.

And because of this
Many very smart people
think that these miracles
with the loaves and fishes
are about food.
And they think this miracle is repeated
because of the importance of food in a subsistence economy.
And that's true,
but that's a human interpretation,
not a Kingdom one.

These stories are about the food,
and they are not about the food.
They are about the Kingdom,
and about God's big plan for all time.

Since the ultimate goal is to sit down with the Father
at a family Table,
everything really is about food,
and the Kingdom.

Next time you read the Bible
and come upon food,
pay attention.

Nothing is wasted in the Bible,
nor is it accidental.
And Jesus
is acting out the Kingdom in these signs.

There is a lot hidden in plain sight
that you will miss
if you concentrate on the food for food's sake.

First let's talk about what Jesus does.
His actions are important.
He is God incarnate—
He's as much the Word when he does something
as when he says something.
All the accounts
take the time to record
what Jesus actually did.
Even Mark,
who tends to be economical with details.

Jesus
took bread,
gave thanks
broke the bread,
and gave it to his disciples,
who then gave it to the crowd.

There is emphasis
on what Jesus did
in these moments,
and it must have been in the center
of the mind of the first believers
to make sure this phrase was in
every retelling of the story.

These are "remembering" details.
There's another place,
recorded in three of the gospels,
where Jesus does this.

And he says that what he does there,
is the SIGN
of the New Covenant in his blood.

Jesus,
took bread,
gave thanks,
broke the bread,
and gave it to his disciples.
Remember.

Maybe these miracles aren't about the food.

But wait,
there's more.

Paul does it too.
In Acts 27:35
Paul
takes bread,
gives thanks,
breaks it and eats.
What he does encourages everyone so much
that they too eat,
and Luke comments
that 276 ate and were satisfied—
from Paul's single piece of bread.

And then in I Corinthians 11:23-24
we hear the most familiar repeat of this phrase:
"For I received from the Lord
what I also handed onto you
that the Lord Jesus
on the night when he was betrayed
took a loaf of bread

and when he had given thanks,
broke it
and said, this is my Body
which is for you."

Paul says the Risen Lord told him this himself.

It is always important to follow these threads in the Bible.
It is a tapestry.
It's not about the food.
It's about the sign.

So Jesus paints this sign
the first time,
on the edge of the Sea of Galilee,
in a Jewish Region.

In the Bible
numbers always mean something.
The Hebrew mind has an interesting relationship with numbers.
They are not just literary devices.
The number five
can relate to the Torah.
It can also relate to grace.
And it can relate to the particular call of the Jewish People
to be a priesthood for the earth under Torah.
In this story, all of this may be true,
because one thousand is always symbolic of multitudes.
five thousand can represent the whole of the Jewish people,
in all times and all places.

And Jesus takes 5 loaves
and breaks them.
Again,
Jesus is symbolically
fulfilling the law
and breaking open Torah
and feeding the Jewish people.

And what about those two fish?
Two always represents separation.
On the second day,
God divided the day from the night.
So in the Jewish mind,
two indicates
a division.

Fish,
and anything from the sea,
is a symbol of Leviathan.
In Jewish mythology,
we will all eat the flesh of Leviathan
at the Resurrection.
This is why the early church ate fish on Friday
not as an act of penance,
but as an act of celebration.
Jesus overcame the devil,
Leviathan
the sea monster,
on the cross.
And so Jesus,
in all these stories,
breaks two fish.
He has ended the separation
between God and humanity,
by destroying the dominion of the devil.
Ever notice that Jesus eats fish after the Resurrection?
He was just showing off.

So Jesus gives thanks,
breaks the bread,
gives it to the disciples,
and they share it among the crowd.
He has the crowd sit,
just like at the Father's table.
They receive, and are served by the apostles.
There is no effort on their part.

And Jesus is very careful to instruct them,
do not let any of it be wasted,
gather it up.

And there were twelve baskets full.
Twelve is the number of the tribes of Israel.
Twelve is the number of the Kingdom.
It is the number of the government of God.

And it is being expressed
through the Messiah
feeding a multitude
who will be priests
for the whole earth.
A new Israel,
made of broken bread.

All these details are signs.
This is beyond conceptual art
and performance art,
and parable,
and even symbol.
It's Incarnation.

And then Jesus,
a few days later,
goes across the lake
to an area full of Gentiles.

And this gets really interesting.
Jesus uses more food to feed fewer people.
In the Gentile region,
Jesus gathers a crowd of 4000.
Yes, Jesus has 4000 Gentile followers.

Again
four means something.
Four is the number that represents the creation,

or the world.
It comes from the four cardinal directions.
Multiply that by one thousand,
and this crowd represents the whole world.
Jesus is coming to feed everybody.
He is not just the Jewish Messiah,
but the Christ for the whole world.

And again
he takes bread.
This time seven loaves,
and "a few small fish."
Seven is the number of fulfillment.
Seven is the number of completion.
God has a plan for the whole world,
not just the Jews,
and the Messiah is going to complete it.
And in the end,
there are seven baskets full.

It is finished.

And then,
as you know,
Jesus
takes bread
and gives thanks,
and breaks it
again on the night he was betrayed.

It is not an accident.
It is not a random use of the same phrase.

Nor is it,
when he does it in Emmaus,
and on the beach by the fire,
and when Paul does it on the ship,
and when Paul reteaches the basics

in the letter to the Corinthians.
Jesus is making Eucharist
and making it clear,
this is the sign
that he is the Messiah,
and the Kingdom is here.
We are going to sit down
with our Father
at Table,
and eat the flesh of Leviathan,
but also the True Bread
from heaven.

The Kingdom of God
is about eating and drinking together
with the Father
and everyone will be satisfied.

From the very beginning
even before the Gospels were written
the Eucharist was the sign.

EAT MY FLESH

I love the Gospel of John.
If I wasn't doing what I do,
talking to artists,
writing emails,
and writing books,
I would spend the rest of my life
writing a commentary on the Gospel of John.

John was an artist.
In the Greek
he uses mininalist language to say big things.
There are several themes you can follow
that give you different perspectives on the story.
And not one detail is an accident.

In the last chapter,
I said that the feeding of the multitude
is the only sign repeated in all the gospels.
And I said it was really about the Eucharist.

John's gospel is the only one
in which Jesus explains the meaning of this sign.
Symbols are amazing things,
but sometimes they need to be tuned
or calibrated,
so you know their true meaning.

Jesus does this in John
chapter 6.

John 6 is one of those places
where the Greek really does make a difference,
and the English translation loses
what the author intended.

                            Prepare to get some new clean lenses.

Our story begins the day after Jesus fed the 5000.
He has gone to the other side of the lake
(by walking on the water).
And the crowd has gone looking for him,
because he gave them food.

They thought it was about the food.

And in John 6:23
we get the first direct clue about
what is going on here.
John wrote after all the other gospels were finished,
and probably after Paul and Peter were dead.
And he was putting the finishing touch
on the story of Jesus.
He filled in
where the others fell short.
And this is one of those places.
The text says,
that they went to the place
where Jesus made Eucharist.

That's what the Greek says.
Your Bible might say,
"the place where the Lord had given thanks."
Not where he fed the multitude,
but where he made Eucharist.

Pay attention.

It's a sign.
It's not about the food.
It's about the Kingdom.

And then Jesus confronts them
and says they are looking for him
because he gave them a free lunch.
And then the crowd replies
by saying Moses gave them Manna,
"what are you going to do to top that?"

And out of this,
Jesus gives us one of the greatest of his
"I am" statements:

I am the Bread of Life
Whoever comes to me
will never be hungry
and whoever believes in me
shall never be thirsty.

Jesus
has tapped into the theme
that I told you about:
Eating and drinking with God.
And he says
that he is the main course.
Remember sacrifice?

And Jesus makes it clear
that you have to believe in him.
You need to believe that he is the Bread from Heaven.
And Jesus again says,
if you have seen him,
you have seen the Father.

Jesus is the sign.

But Jesus is not just asking us to
"believe in our hearts
with every eye closed,
and every head bowed."
Jesus is not asking you to come forward
at the crusade and talk to the nice counselor.
Jesus is not asking you to make a mental commitment.

No,
he is asking you to eat his flesh.
Believing and doing are one.

"I am the Living Bread
that came down from heaven.
Whoever eats of this bread
will live forever,
and the bread that I give
for the life of the world
is my flesh."

The Greek mindset
wants to keep faith
and belief
in your head
where it can remain impersonal.
And because of this,
we have developed a
"gnostic" or "dualistic"
understanding of Christianity.

Jesus is about to mess with all that.
And here is where the Greek matters.

Beginning in John 6:53
Jesus changes the word that he used
for eating.
Up until then,
he used the polite word for "eat."

And he knew rightly
that his hearers,
and people up to the present day
could "spiritualize"
what he said,
to mean some mental
exercise in belief.

But Jesus isn't talking about food,
or belief in an abstract sense.
He is talking about the goal of the Father,
to re-establish his Kingdom
built on organic relationships
within his own family.

And Jesus
is the sacrifice,
the Lamb,
the Bread,
and the Life.

Jesus uses a word here,
"abide"
that he will use again
in the context of Passover
and the first Eucharist.
Abiding is not trying to be in the Presence of God,
Abiding is about eating
around a Table.

And Jesus
to make his point
uses a variant of the word
"trago" to describe
eating his flesh.
It was very offensive,
and many people left him.

Trago,
is the word for
chew,
gnaw,
rip apart with your teeth,
or feed upon.

The image it conveys
is a pack of lions
feeding upon
a fresh kill.

Pretty grim,
grisly,
and graphic.

Jesus was going to force them
out of their spiritualized religion,
and into flesh and blood reality.
His body is going to be ripped apart.
His flesh is going to be torn.
His blood is going to be spilled.
And you will need to eat it,
if you want to have
eternal life.

Listen to my rendering
with the original intent:

Very truly I tell you,
unless you chew on the
flesh of the Son of Man,
and drink his blood,
you have no life within you.
Those who gnaw upon
my flesh, and drink my blood
have eternal life
and I will raise them up
on the last day.

Those who feed upon
my flesh
and drink my blood
abide in me
and I
in them.
Whover
devours me
will live
because of me.
Whoever feeds on this bread
will live forever.

Yes,
they thought he was a cannibal.
And the early church was accused of this practice
for hundreds of years.
It is right here.
It's not about mental belief
or agreement.
It's about gathering around the Body of the Lord
and receiving nourishment,
in the most graphic sense imaginable.

God is offensive.
In fact,
God often uses offense to reveal our hearts.

One day I was having a conversation with God,
and I asked Him,
"Lord, why did you make all those people
laugh at Toronto?"

And the Lord replied,
"I wanted to offend people,
to get them ready for what I am about to do."

And I said,
"Lord, what are you about to do?"

"Really offend people,
I am about to restore the Eucharist
and the Sacraments
to the Church."

It's funny how when I talk about some of these things
the first response
always seems to be
"I don't believe that."

Jesus said to believe
means to eat.
Not to agree.
We have gotten some very important things wrong.

Jesus fed
five thousand
to fulfill His calling as the Jewish Messiah
and four thousand
to complete his mission as Saviour of the World.

Jesus was creating signs,
and those signs pointed to one sign,
eating his flesh
and drinking his blood
as a sign of the covenant.

It was all about the Kingdom.

COVENANT

So if Jesus was making signs,
they must have been pointing toward something.
The Bible is a forward looking book.

There is a forward glance throughout the story.

And every time God
does something new,
there is a promise of something better later.
Every time God does something new
He does it by making a covenant.
At one level covenants are legal agreements,
but remember:
God is the Most Relational Being in the Universe.

A Covenant is about defining a relationship.

And every covenant comes with a promise
of the benefits of this redefined relationship;
and every covenant comes with a sign.

We often see covenants in a negative light:
what we are supposed to do,
but honestly,
God sees them in a positive light.

God will never flood the earth again,
and Noah is given a rainbow.

Abraham will be the Father of Many Nations   .
and his people will be circumcised.

Under Moses Israel will be a holy Nation,
and carry a moral code to the rest of the earth,
and be blessed with a day of rest.
And that covenant with Moses
was celebrated and renewed every year
at the Passover.
It was about re-membering.
Remember?

And even in that covenant with Moses
there is the forward glance,
the looking toward another Prophet
who will exceed and fulfill
all that God did through Moses.

There is the forward glance to the new and better covenant
where there is no longer an outward law,
but the Lawgiver
will live inside
and give us a new heart,
and a new Spirit.

Through Ezekiel
God says he will make a new covenant
with the House of Israel.
He will take away our hearts of stone,
and give us hearts of flesh.
We will be His people,
and He will be our God.
And God will wash us with clean water,
and put His Spirit within us,
and open our graves.

That's the sign,
that the dead would be raised.

When we come to the end of the Gospels,
Jesus says something interesting.

"I eagerly long
to celebrate
this Passover
with you."

For three years
he has been preaching the message of his Kingdom,
and performing signs
to point the way to the Kingdom.

And in one night,
Jesus takes the national holiday of Israel,
and he redefines it.
His entire ministry
is going to culminate
in this one act.

He takes what was about them,
and makes it about Him.

He simplifes and amplifies
Passover.

In a normal Seder there are four cups of wine.
There is also a ceremony with three pieces of Matzah—
unleavened bread pierced with holes.

The seder begins with these three pieces of bread,
stacked in the middle of the table.
And the second one,
the one in the middle,
is broken.

That broken one is hidden and found.
After the meal,
the broken one is eaten.

And Jesus
after the meal
takes that broken Matzah
and he says:

"This is my Body,
broken for you.
Eat this in remembrance of me."
And he takes the bread,
gives thanks,
breaks it,
and gives it to the disciples.

And then he takes the third cup
from the service,
the cup of Redemption,
and he says,
"this cup is my Blood of the New Covenant."

Did you get that?

God is doing a new thing.
And when God does a new thing
God makes a covenant.
This covenant is being made
not with the blood of a bull or a goat.
This covenant is being made with blood
shed from Jesus.
And this cup
is the New Covenant.
And the sign of the new covenant
will be:
You will receive power when the Holy Spirit
comes upon you
and you will be my witnesses.

Jesus is making a covenant with us,
and this bread
and this wine
are the covenant.
You can't separate the covenant
from the Eucharist.
The early church knew this.
That is why Sunday mattered.
It was about renewing the covenant,
not once a year at the temple
but once a week in the Body.

Before Jesus went to the Cross
he made a covenant,
an agreement with you.
That agreement
was
that God would dwell in you,
and you would receive a new heart
and a new Spirit.
You would be his people,
and he would be your God.
And this would be the sign,
He would open their graves.
He sealed it with his own body,
through death and resurrection,
and afterward
gave us the Holy Spirit.

The covenant was made the night he redefined Passover.
And the cross and resurrection
sealed it.

It wasn't just a memorial of something in the past.
It was a remembering,
a reconnecting,
and a weekly renewing of that covenant.

I still find it amazing
that the church existed without a Bible for quite a while.
The earliest New Testament books
they estimate
came twenty years
after the church began.

And the Bible as a whole
really didn't take the shape we recognize
for several centuries.
Yes, I said centuries.

But we know
that the Eucharist
came first.
It was the breaking of the bread,
in Acts,
and in the Gospels,
and in Paul's letters.
This was a new thing.
These folks understood that.

It was the last thing Jesus told us to do,
on the night before he died.

We have lost so much.
God made a new Covenant with Israel
and all Humanity,
and that Covenant
is the legal foundation for the Kingdom.
And the covenant was bread and wine.

And Jesus,
even in the New Covenant
said he was looking forward:
to drinking the last cup of Passover,
in the Kingdom,
when He comes again.

Once you wrap your head around this:
that it is all about
eating and drinking
in the Presence of God,
then you see it everywhere in the Bible.

It is why God ate with the elders of Israel
on the mountain,
and didn't harm them.

It is why Melchizedek
offered bread and wine.

It is why Elijah could live for forty days
on one loaf of bread.

And David ate the bread of the Presence.

This Covenant
is about
sitting down in the
Presence of the Father,
and eating together
as a new creation.

PRESENCE

Whenever I
am in Buffalo, New York
on a Sunday morning,
I attend Saints Peter and Paul
in Hamburg.

It is your average Catholic parish
in an average suburb,
not far from where my family lives,
and very near the house
where my grandmother grew up.

One Sunday
there was a new priest
and he invited all the children to come forward and
gather near the altar.

And as he was preparing the table for the Eucharist,
he looked at the children
and he said,
"Pay attention.
When I hold my hands over the bread and wine
you are going to feel something.
That's the Holy Spirit."

He knew,
as I do,
and Luther,
and Wesley did,
that Jesus is really present.
It is something you only get to experience
when you celebrate at the altar.

It happens every time.

The first time that we get a glimpse of this mystery
is in the story
of the pair on the road to Emmaus.

It says Jesus
"opened their minds to understand the Scriptures"
that "their hearts burned" with heat as they walked along the road,
and that "they knew Him in the breaking of the Bread."

It is important to note that Luke says they
testified to the Resurrection
and to knowing Jesus in the Breaking of the Bread.

They were having an experience of the Holy Spirit.

In John's Gospel,
on the same night,
Jesus appeared to them
after walking through a locked door,
and breathed on them
and said,

"Receive the Holy Spirit."

You cannot understand the
mystery of the
Presence of Jesus
in the Eucharist,

unless you understand the Presence of Jesus
in the Holy Spirit.
And you cannot understand the Presence of Jesus
in the Eucharist,
unless you recognize the Holy Spirit's Presence
in the believers around you at the Table.
Remember,
this is still
all about relationship.

The healing of relationships may be
the most important thing
the Holy Spirit
does
in the life
of believers.

This is why
Jesus, at the last supper in John's gospel,
doesn't explain Holy Communion,
he explains the Promise of the Holy Spirit,
and how to live in him—
abide.
And like I said earlier,
abiding in Jesus
is coming together
around the table.
And eating His Body and Blood.
That's what Jesus said.
John 6,
remember?

It is also why Paul,
in I Corinthians 11
first corrects how they celebrate the Lord's Supper together,
and then corrects their practice of life in the Holy Spirit.
Although many stop reading in the middle of the sentence
when Paul instructs them to examine themselves;

Paul tells them to examine themselves
so that they discern the Lord's Body
in the Eucharist.
The body on the table,
and the body gathered around it.

And then Paul goes right into the supernatural gifts of the Spirit,
speaking in tongues and prophecy,
and then LOVE.
It is all about relationships,
and life in the Spirit.
They cannot be divided.
Paul knew
that the
Person
Presence
and Power
of Jesus
through the Holy Spirit
was in operation
whenever we gather
to feast in His name.

In the book of Exodus,
Moses was commanded
to place bread on a table,
in the Holy Place,
and it was to sit there all week.
The Priests were to consume it
on the Sabbath.

The rest of the week,
it was there as a sign of the Presence.
In fact, in Hebrew,
it is called
"Presence Bread."

This bread was so important,
that it was to be on the table,

even when they moved from one place to another.
A picture is worth a thousand words,
and when you read it all through the wrong lens,
you miss all this performance
and conceptual art.
For three thousand years,
God has been showing us the same thing.

You may have seen pictures of the priests
carrying the ark,
but I don't think you have ever seen pictures
of them carrying the table with the bread.

                                                    I never have.

This bread
is a prophetic
sign
that Jesus would one day be present
with us
by the Holy Spirit,
and whenever we gathered
to share Bread and Wine.

The Word became flesh.
And now
through the Word
and Holy Spirit,
the Word becomes bread
and we receive the Word
in our own bodies.

And it is a mystery.
And it changes things.

For about ten years,
we had a team that would go and pray on location.
We called these little adventures
healing the land assignments.

We went places where sin had been committed,
and where a curse had taken hold.
For the record,
the land gets cursed through
the shedding of innocent blood,
idolatry,
sexual immorality,
breaking of covenants,
and the moving of boundary stones.

We would go and confess the sins
of those who went before us,
and celebrate communion.
And most importantly,
break the bread.
We found that breaking the bread
was important.

In the first few months of Belonging House,
a murder happened on our block.
It was a big deal,
because ours was a fairly stable
middle class neighborhood with kids
and families.
The murder happened near the school.

After our Thursday night meeting,
our group went and prayed at the location of the murder.
It was a gloomy night,
and you could tell,
the neighborhood had changed.
People were afraid to leave their houses,
and they were afraid the neighborhood was going to
become unsafe.

We took the bread
which had been consecrated during our evening meeting
back at the
house,
and said a simple prayer,
"Lamb of God,
who takes away the sin of the world,
have mercy on us.
Lamb of God,
who takes away the sin of the world,
have mercy on us.
Lamb of God,
who takes away the sin of the world,
Grant us your peace."
and broke the bread.

Immediately a bird began to sing,
the sky cleared and it became a beautiful moonlit night,
and people gradually began coming out into the street to walk,
just like before the murder.

After this,
I read a story about Pope John Paul II
visiting the Nazi concentration camp at Auschwitz.
That day he celebrated the Eucharist.
And at the moment he broke the bread,
all the birds in the trees began to sing.
They had not sung there since before the war.

They knew Him in the Breaking of the Bread.
The Eucharist isn't a
magic weapon in your intercessory toolbox.
The Eucharist
is the Presence of Jesus,
and He is the King of the Kingdom.
Wherever the King goes,
things come into order.

In the beginning of this book
I said that there are things that are mysteries.

We don't know it all.
One gets into trouble when they say they have the answers.
The Eastern Orthodox Churches
do not know how Jesus is present,
but they know that when they pray
and ask the Holy Spirit
to come over this bread and wine,
He is.

Jesus said he would be with us.
His presence is tangible,
and changes things,
and more importantly,
changes lives.

BODY

You can't help being Jewish.

If you are,
you are.

It's a matter of genetics,
culture,
and history.

> There is an old saying,
> "Wherever there are two Jews,
> there are
> three opinions."

Throughout Jewish history
it is striking how many
factions,
sects,
and
schools of thought
have existed.

At the time of Jesus we know there were at least
five
distinct
schools of Judaism,
and within those there were undoubtedly sub-groups.

And yet,
in the face of the Romans,
they were one.

They were one
because they had shared ancestors.
They were a nation
because they were also a family.
Differing opinions,
sects,
factions,
and sub-groups
cannot change that reality.

Before
the night before Jesus died,
in order to be in relationship
with God,
you had to be born into the nation of Israel,
or you had to become a proselyte.
That meant you needed
to receive a form of ritual bath
and you had to
be circumcised
if you were male.

That's commitment.

After the New Covenant,
the Cross,
the Resurrection,
and the Outpouring of the Holy Spirit,
if you wanted to have a relationship with God,
you needed to be
in
Jesus.

In Jesus,
not
in Israel.

That meant
receiving a ritual bath,
just like Israel before,
but then
sitting down at the Father's Table
and feeding on the
Bread of Life.

To be in Jesus
meant to eat His Body.
You are what you eat,
and so you have now become
a member of the Body of Christ.

And it is this metaphor
Body,
that dominates the New Testament.

Rightly so,
Paul goes from
1 Corinthians 11
and the discourse on the Lord's Supper,
to the next three chapters of the letter
talking about how a Body functions.

I said this in the last chapter,
but it is so important it bears repeating.

Paul goes from the Lord's Supper
to the supernatural gifts
given by God
to make this Body function in the world.
Paul says to us,
if you do not see the Body of Jesus
in the Eucharist
you will not see the Body of Christ all around you
in the community.

And because of this
the life has stopped flowing.
People are sick
and dying
in a community
called to bring life
and healing
to the world.

As the Jews were "in Israel"
so are we
"in Christ."

By eating his flesh
and drinking his blood,
we become what we eat.
We become the Body of Christ.
And that reality
cannot
be impacted by
differing opinions,
differing theologies,
and
differing ways of doing things.

But bodies have different organs
and different parts of the body do different things.
You don't all have to be prophets,
or evangelists,
or write,
or preach,
or serve the poor,
or teach.
You are already in the Body,
and what comes naturally
through the ease of the Holy Spirit
is probably what you are called to do.

We have gotten so many important things wrong.
And the Christianity we experience
is inadequate.

Most of my Christian experience
has been in churches that celebrated Communion
at least weekly.
One church
in particular
was part of a global
move of the Holy Spirit.
We were a bit crazy at times,
but we had
what one friend has called,
a warm
cozy
welcoming
atmosphere.
Although things did get out-of-hand at times,
I remember that
there were not a lot of
relationship
issues
among the people.

After that season,
I began doing work
with ministries outside my own
denomination.

                                                    I still do.

And one thing that strikes me
as I work with
evangelicals,
and independent charismatic
churches,
is the brittleness
I find
in relationships.

A lot of people spend their time
being "prophetic"
and confronting one another.
There is a lot of church hopping,
church splitting,
and a lot of people breaking fellowship
over the finest point of doctrine.

The life doesn't flow.

Christian Unity,
as I hear it taught
and promoted,
is an idol.

I've seen more sin,
more misinterpretation of Scripture,
and more emotional manipulation
in the name of Unity
than any other
topic.

What people mean
by Unity
is agreement.
Jesus
never called you
to agree with someone.
He called you to Himself.

He said,
take up your cross and follow me.
Not Paul
Cephas,
Apollos,
Luther,
Calvin,
Wesley,

Pope John Paul II,
Pope Francis,
or anybody.
Follow Me.

Eat of my flesh,
and drink my blood,
so that you will have life within you.

Unity in the New Testament
is found in the Holy Spirit,
and outwardly expressed when we gather around the Lord's Body.
As Jesus said,
where the body is,
the birds gather.
Crows go where the food is.
One beggar tells another
the place where he found bread.

We are called to gather around him.
And discern the Lord's body
in bread and wine,
and
discern the Lord's body
in the motley group of people
in our midst.

It doesn't matter
if you agree on politics,
or intellectual pursuits.
It matters that you are in Him
and He is in you.

We are one,
because of one loaf,
not because of one opinion.

LITTLE CUPS

In the 1970's
my seminary started a
Christian music festival
as a response to Woodstock.

It was called "Ichthus."

It happened every year in late April
in Kentucky.
And like Woodstock,
it usually meant camping in the mud for three days.

The highlight of the festival was a service of the Lord's Supper,
where about 10,000 attendees shared little cubes of bread,
and little cups of grape juice,
together.

And for many who came to Ichthus,
that was their moment with Jesus,
and their lives changed.

When you have 10,000 little plastic cups,
and you hear them all popped open at the same moment,
that "pop" is actually quite a sound.
And you realize, you are not alone.

In 1995 Ichthus celebrated its Twenty-fifth anniversary.
And there was a record crowd.
Part of my job, because I worked for the chapel,
was to help organize this communion service.

We normally
planned on 10,000 little cups.
This year, we prepared 12,000.
The crowd was estimated at over 20,000.
The local authorities were very concerned.

So, how did we do this?
We filled little plastic take-away containers with grape juice.
And we filled plastic bags with pre-cut little squares of bread.
and we put these in cardboard boxes.
I believe each box contained enough for 100 people.
When the moment came,
we asked the crowd to join hands,
and we walked through the rows until the elements were gone.

Although most of the volunteers did not know our situation,
I knew we only had enough for about half the crowd.

And so we prayed,
gave thanks,
and made our way out into the multitude.
And when it was over,
most of the boxes had about 25-30 cups of grape juice left over.
The proof was in the leftovers.

It was a miracle.

But here is the kicker.

Unlike when Jesus fed the multitudes,
and instructed them to be careful with the leftovers,
the volunteers tossed the boxes aside.
Some of the cups spilled out onto the ground.

Other volunteers threw the boxes and kicked them out of the way.
Others put their boxes right into the garbage dumpsters.

I had witnessed a miracle
and the utter disregard for communion
in the same moment.

Little cups are a new innovation in the church.
They were invented in the late 19th Century in the United States
by the Methodists.
The Methodists had become a church
committed to the Temperance movement.

                                                        That is, no booze.

And to be consistent,
they pursued a way to take wine out of communion.
A Methodist finally discovered
a way to prevent grape juice
from fermenting,
and this was developed for church.
But there was a problem.
Everyone drinking unfermented grape juice from one cup
was a way to spread germs and disease.
We can't have that.
And so,
little glass cups were born.

                                                (My dear friend,
                        the Reverend Doctor Jennifer Woodruff-Tait
                                wrote an excellent book on this.)

And rather than one loaf,
and one cup,
making One Body,
we had many little individual cups,
and many little individual cubes of bread.
A bunch of little individuals.
No breaking of bread,
it was already cut up in the kitchen.

And not to be outdone,
soon enterprising folks
learned you could prepackage cut up bread.
And make little plastic disposable cups.
No washing!
No recruiting volunteers.

And then,
another enterprising man
(it was a man, and I knew him)
decided to alter the rip off coffee creamer
and turn that into a communion cup,
with a little wafer on top.
"Because communion is taking too much time."

Do you see where this is going?

McDonald's is classier.

Remember the point:
God wants you to eat with Him
forever
at the ultimate
dinner party.
The best
of the best
of the best.

I am going to end this book
on a high and inspirational note.
In order to do that,
I have to give you the correction part of this book now.
My first draft of this book
had to be destroyed.
I was very angry
as I thought of all the abuses
I have seen
at the Communion Table.

All the bad teaching,
lack of training,
disposable communion sets,
and commercialization,
have resulted in pastors who do not
even know the basics of what is going on.
Many don't know even the basic scriptures about
the Eucharist,
and have never been taught.
And they see this ignorance as a positive.
It makes them better than the "Catholics."

I've seen churches throw the bread on the ground,
crowds pushing others to get at it,
and guests and vistors (me, I'm afraid)
not even get a crumb.
I've seen youth pastors
bless takeout pizza
and Pepsi cola
and call it the Body and Blood of Christ.
And then everyone went and played Ping-Pong.
These are seminary trained leaders,
and the seminary taught them to do it.

(I was in the class.)

When you study the history of the Eucharist,
you find that whenever an error comes into the church
concerning Holy Communion,
about a hundred years later
that error takes root in the church as a movement.

We are there, friends.

So an innocent innovation
that had some commercial possibilities,
has resulted in
a narcissistic,
individualistic,
form of Christianity.

A church where everything is for sale,
and marketing is seen as spiritual credibility.
Where your choices in life,
and as a church organization,
have no relationship to the rest of the Body of Christ—
because there is no longer a body,
only individual disconnected parts.
Competition,
marketing,
and the free market
have prevailed.

Cheap,
fast,
programmed,
and all about my needs,
has become the creed.

And even brothers and sisters
who are beginning to get a new appreciation
for the Eucharist,
only see it as a tool in their "arsenal of intercession."

Rather than this being
about the Father
and the Kingdom,
Holy Communion has become something
tacked on during the service
that we hopefully can keep short
so it doesn't take too much time from
the promo videos
about the
group study,
building program,
pastor's new book,
or
youth trip to the mountains.

Rather than decently and in order,
we have attendants at the end of every row of seats,
with garbage bags
to collect
your little plastic
cups.

There wasn't even a prayer.
"Next time, can we find a way to make it more meaningful?"

We have gotten some very important things wrong.
Paul said
that because you have gotten the Eucharist wrong,
you are sick.
Some of you are dying.
You have held the primary thing
Jesus left us
as a sign of his covenant
in contempt.

And when I share
these thoughts with my brothers and sisters,
their religious pride,
and self-righteous attitude rises up.
"I'm not a Catholic, and I am not going back to the Middle ages."
I'm not talking Catholic.
I'm talking Bible.
I'm talking New Covenant.
I'm talking Body of Christ.
I'm talking King and the Kingdom.

It is time to metanoia.
It is time to change your thinking.
This is not just a memorial
that we have once a month.
It is not about you and Jesus in the back of the prayer room all alone.
It is not okay to make the Body and Blood of Jesus disposable.
Jesus did not say pizza and Pepsi are his Body and Blood.

When you don't recognize His Body,
you don't see the Body all around you.

Maybe God
is multiplying
bread and wine
all around you.
Have you tossed it aside?
Have you held the holy
with contempt?
Open your eyes
and see the glory of God.
May you see Jesus
in the Breaking of the Bread.

Father,
I ask that you open the mind of my friend
reading this book.
May you revolutionize their thinking,
and produce a reformation
that changes the world.

This isn't about rules.
It's about grace.
The King
who was with you in the courtroom
is fighting for you,
to come and sit down with his Father
and feast in his Presence
from one cup
in one Body.

That's a reason to rejoice.

EVERYTHING

There was a time
when we never knew
what would happen next
at our church.

Sometimes
you just get accustomed
to expecting the unexpected.

One Sunday
we had come to the part of the service
when everyone
came forward to receive
Holy Communion.

In those days we had many visitors,
because our church had become
known for healing the sick.

Unusual things often happened,
but rarely did something happen
that stopped the show.

One Sunday,
a stranger in our midst
came forward.

And when she received the bread,
and it touched her lips,
she let out a blood-curdling scream.

Everyone, and everything
stopped.
The woman was not alone.
She was accompanied by her translator.
She had been born deaf
and never went anywhere
without someone who could
use sign language to interpret.

The interpreter quickly motioned
to the hysterical woman
to find out what had happened.

"I can hear."

Jesus Christ
is the same
yesterday,
today,
and
forever.

And somehow
God became a man
and man
has become bread.

And everything that bread and wine is
for us
is Jesus.
Food,
nutrition,
fuel,
strength,

joy,
inebriation,
celebration,
warmth,
medicine,
and
life.

Jesus said,
do this
in remembrance of me.

When we encounter the Eucharist
we encounter the same
Spirit
that raised Jesus from the dead.
It's the life
that Jesus promised in the Vine.

All that Jesus taught about the Holy Spirit,
in the Upper Room
he taught
after they had shared the broken Bread
and the poured out Wine.

It is through the Holy Spirit
that we are adopted
as children
and we cry
Abba, Father.

Here we are again.
That's the point.

We are called to gather around one Table
and be seated with our Father.
A new Creation.
A new Identity.
A sense of Value.
And a place to Belong.

Over the past 30-odd years
I have seen relationships heal around the table.
I've seen bodies heal.
I've seen people get free from cycles of trauma
and addiction.

I have watched as the Kingdom
made itself perfectly real.

We do so many things
Jesus never asked us to do.
Bible studies,
programs,
buildings,
music,
theology,
and
institutions.
And the one thing he asked us to do
on the night before he died,
we ignore.

God has so much more for you
than you think.

My personal attitude
toward Holy Communion
changed
after one of those private
conversations you have
with a great saint.

In my youth I knew many old
saintly evangelists.
These were men who traveled during the
Pentecostal
Holiness
and Healing Revivals
of the mid-20th Century.

I was just a kid,
but I knew these men had something I did not.

One of these men
had been the personal chauffeur
for Smith Wigglesworth,
when he was on an American preaching tour.

For you who might not know,
Smith Wiggleworth
was an early Pentecostal
miracle worker.
He raised the dead
and healed the sick
on a pretty regular basis.
And Smith Wigglesworth
got his start
in the Salvation Army.

And just as a point of fact,
the Salvation Army does not celebrate
Holy Communion.

As I was saying,
my dear friend
enjoyed telling me what it was like to live
day by day
with Smith Wigglesworth.

You really never know someone until you travel with them.

Brother Bill,
(that was his name)
told me one outrageous story
about Smith Wigglesworth
interrupting a funeral,
and raising an embalmed man from the dead.

Yes, embalming fluid
and cotton stuffing,
and all.

Twenty years later
one of Wiggleworth's last eyewitnesses
confirmed that story.
Smith had done it more than once.

And here is the kicker.
Every morning
at five o'clock,
Smith Wiggleworth
woke Bill up from a sound sleep,
and made him take
communion.

It turns out,
that was the secret of Smith Wigglesworth's power.
He began
every day
by reconnecting with the Source.

Yes,
there was prayer,
and there was Bible reading,
and there was fellowship with other believers,
and there was worship and praise.
But first there was
the Bread of Life.

It is all very practical.

We make everything so spiritual
and so ethereal.
God wants you
to chew on his flesh
and drink his blood.

So that you may have life within you.
Jesus
knew
that something about eating and drinking
together in the presence of God
said something about the Kingdom.

As it says in the Passover service:
All who are hungry,
come and eat;
all who are needy,
come and celebrate.
This year we are slaves;
next year we will be free.

And in this bread
and this wine
we encounter a broken body.
We encounter a cup of blessing.
We encounter our brothers and sisters.
We encounter the reminder
that Jesus died
and is coming again.
We encounter
so much.

Yes,
this is still a book for artists.
Over the past two thousand years,
no single thing
has inspired more art
than the Eucharist.

It was art
that adorned the catacombs
where Christians
gathered
to eat Bread and Wine.

A whole symbolic system
fish,
pelicans,
peacocks,
shepherds,
anchors,
wheat,
grapes,
and
on and on,
developed.

When I was a student,
learning about the theatre
and reading about acting,
I learned that out of the Mass
western theatre emerged.
The re-enactment of the last supper
became the precursor
of the most important
form of art in our day.

I believe God wants to reawaken
the creativity
of the Body of Christ,
and it will begin with Jesus.

Jesus is the centre,
not your church
or your theology.

There are a million books on the Eucharist.
At least a million,
probably more.

I have spent 30 years pondering this mystery.
I have seen a fair share of God encounters,
and miracles.

And yet,
I haven't touched
even the depths
of the Covenant,
and the Grace,
and Wholeness that is ours
in the Eucharist.

As Jesus said
He is the Bread that came down from Heaven.
He is infinite,
limitless,
goodness,
and
grace.

Rather than inadequate,
Jesus is fully adequate.

Here is something someone wrote
in the fourth century.
It seems to sum it up:
> Hope, Life, Way
> Salvation,
> Understanding,
> Wisdom, Light,
> Judge, Door,
> Most High, King,
> Precious Stone, Prophet, Priest,
> Messiah, Sabaoth, Teacher, Spouse,
> Mediator, Scepter, Dove, Hand,
> Stone, Son, Emmanuel,
> Vineyard, Shepherd, Sheep,
> Peace, Root, Vinestock,
> Olive Tree, Source, Wall,
> Lamb, Victim, Lion,
> Intercessor, Word, Man,
> Net, Rock, House—Jesus Christ is Everything.

THE LAST CUP

So to recap,
there is a thesis
to this little book.

To sit down with the Father
around a table
and have dinner
together as a redeemed and restored family.

                                          Full stop.

I mentioned earlier,
Jesus blessed the third cup
during Passover
and said,
"This cup
was the New Covenant
in my blood."

That third cup is the cup of Redemption:
"I will redeem you with an outstretched arm."

I also said,
that the Bible is forward looking.
God is always forward looking.
And Jesus begins
his New Covenant
with a forward glance.

He tells us
that he will not drink the last cup
until he establishes his kingdom.

And if you look carefully,
you see
in the gospels,
Jesus never drinks wine again
after the Last Supper.

That last cup is the cup of Praise.
And with it comes this promise:

                                            I will
                                        take you
                              as my own people.

Isaiah said
One day
all things will be made right
on the Holy Mountain
and all the people of God will gather
and eat and drink
and be satisfied.

Paul said
we eat this bread
and drink this cup
to proclaim the Lord's death
until he comes again.

We are always looking forward
to the fullness
of who we really are
when the token
of bread and wine
becomes the real thing.
When there is no longer any separation from God
and no separation from each other.

We are whole.
One with the Father
and the Son,
and the Holy Spirit.

A Body,
a temple,
and a family.

Jesus Christ
is God in the flesh.
And God first revealed himself as Creator.
And Jesus
became a man
the Image of God,
the B'Tzelem Elohim.
The Bezalel of a new Temple of the Holy Spirit.
You and me.

We are temples of the Holy Spirit.
We are His masterpieces,
little pieces
from the One Loaf.

And one day,
Jesus will gather all of us together
and we will be as one.

Until then
we must do what he said:
take bread,
give thanks,
break it
and give it to the world.

A sign,
a wonder,
a work of Incarnation.

We artists and creative people
are called to make culture.

And those of us who are disciples of Jesus
are called to make the cultures of this earth
like the culture of heaven.

We are called to set places at the Table of the Father
for those who are hungry,
lonely,
lost,
and
afraid.

The Father has no limits on the size of his family.

The whole point of the Christian faith is this:

That we would sit down
at the Father's table together.

One day,
we will be drinking that last cup with Jesus.
The Bible ends with this:

Hallelujah!
For the Lord our God the Almighty reigns.
Let us rejoice and be glad
and give God the glory,
for the Marriage of the Lamb has come
and his bride has made herself ready. (Revelation 19:6b-7)

And the angel said to me,
"Write this:
Blessed are those
who are invited
to the marriage supper
of the Lamb." (Revelation 19:9)

[Jerusalem's] gates will never be shut by day—
there will be no night there.
People will bring
into it
the glory and honor
of the nations. (Revelation 21:25-26)

The Spirit and the Bride say 'Come.'
And let everyone who hears say, 'Come.'
And let everyone who is thirsty come.
Let anyone who wishes take the water of life as a gift. (Revelation 22:17)

When we eat this bread,
and drink this cup
we are declaring the mystery
that Jesus died,
Jesus rose again from the dead,
and we are going to go to an eternal wedding feast with him.

And your job,
as a living member of his body,
is to be broken bread
and poured out wine
as a sign and wonder.

A living work of art,
using art and culture
to prepare the way for the coming of the Lord.

No eye has seen,
no ear has heard,
and no mind can comprehend,
what God has prepared for us,
or what can happen
when we walk in our full
unbroken
identity
as sons and daughters,

waiting to join
in a celebration
at the Father's Table.

Hallelujah.

Father,
I bless the person
who has taken the time
to read this book.
Holy Spirit,
give them wisdom
revelation,
and an ever increasing knowledge
of the Love of God.
May they too
sit down with me
at the Father's Table
and rejoice together
that we are one Body,
just as there
is one loaf.
Through Jesus Christ
the Living Bread.
Amen.

ABOUT THE AUTHOR

Christ John Otto is the founder of Belonging House, a relational and spiritual fellowship of artists and creative people who are called to build Jesus a throne in the earth.

For more information,
please go to Belonginghouse.org